Exploring A Career As A Virtual Assistant

By: Jessica Maes

2nd Edition

©2012 – Jessica Maes

Contents:

2nd Edition Forward

When I first wrote and published this book in 2009 I was actively running a Virtual Assistance business. You will read all about why I originally wrote this book in Chapter 2, and that reason hasn't changed, of course.

However, it's 2012 now and much HAS changed in the Virtual Assistance industry as well as in my business. For starters, I no longer operate a full time Virtual Assistance business. And not because the VA industry isn't working anymore—quite the contrary. For me, I found a marketing niche that I decided to spend all of my time consulting on.

I now consult on a type marketing automation software called Infusionsoft®. I learned about Infusionsoft in the course of working with my Virtual Assistant clients, so this information is relevant to this book in more ways than explaining what I'm up to. I will talk more about Infusionsoft® within the context of the Virtual Assistance industry in Chapter 7.

I feel a book like this—one that explains the basics of the Virtual Assistance industry—is still very helpful, important and now that I have updated it—relevant. People continue to be searching for jobs and businesses continue to operate more creatively to control costs. Virtual Assistants are very much in demand—I would say even more so than 2-3 years ago.

I'm not going to point out what updates I have made to this book because that would be confusing. If you are reading this book for the first time, you will not even realize that it's a 2nd Edition. If you read the 1st Edition, I recommend you reread the book and not overanalyze what is different. Put it this way: THIS version of this book is what is relevant

NOW. I promise it will change again, but for now, this is a great resource to help you decide if starting a Virtual Assistance business is a good fit for you.

I am delighted to have updated this book. It remains my passion to help people help themselves.

To your success!

Jessica Maes
-February, 2012

Chapter 1

Introduction

Congratulations! Sitting down to read this book and learn about the Virtual Assistance industry is a step in the direction of operating your very own sustainable small business. It's a big deal, and you should be proud of yourself for even considering taking this leap (starting a business is not just a step, it's a **leap**!).

By the end of this book you will have a clear understanding about the Virtual Assistance industry and many of the ins and outs of starting and operating a Virtual Assistance practice. This **is not** a step-by-step guide to setting up and running a Virtual Assistance practice. There are already established, reputable options for this that I will mention later in the book so that you can explore the options further on your own.

This book will cover exactly what the title says: **Exploring**. We will explore the industry, explore examples of what makes a successful Virtual Assistance practice operate, explore some of the in-demand niche opportunities that are available to Virtual Assistants these days and explore what to do to take the next step in starting your Virtual Assistance business. **Note: This book is geared toward administrative professionals that are not currently Virtual Assistants.**

Please keep an open mind about this information. Many people assume that all work from home opportunities are not all that they appear to be (i.e. a scam). I'm here to tell you that yes, many work from home opportunities that you see on the Internet or stapled to telephone poles around town **are** too good to be true. However, Virtual Assistance is not in that category. All of the information that I share in this book is true and accurate and most often rooted in my own experiences—personally and with others.

So sit back, and get ready to be wowed—and hopefully inspired. You are about to learn about one of the best careers you probably have never heard of: Virtual Assistance. Most people find information about this business model fascinating, and I hope you do too. I wish you all the best!

Jessica Maes
-2012

Chapter 2
Why I Wrote This Book

I feel it's important to share part of my career journey with you as I'm pretty sure that something in my story will undoubtedly ring true for you too. I spent a lot of years thinking my journey was unique, but I have learned that we are all a lot more alike than we are different. The details that you read here may not be identical, but feelings are universal, and I'm confident you will be able to relate as you hear my story.

Back in 2005 I had two jobs. I was working part-time operating my own real estate sales brokerage (it sounds much fancier than it was!) and full-time as a claims examiner at a large insurance company. My husband and I were expecting a baby boy that May, and the plan was that I would stay home full-time to care for him once he arrived.

As is often the case in life, things didn't go exactly as planned. My baby was born in March. I left work on a Friday for the weekend and never returned. Looking back, I believe that the sudden and massive shift of events was traumatic, and probably played a role in what happened next.

In full disclosure, I know that I was extremely fortunate to have the opportunity to stay home and raise our child. When I took off my parent hat and assessed my life, however, I felt tremendously isolated in my new role, my new purpose in life. I no longer earned a dime, and my entire day revolved around caring for a baby. I love my family, but I also love myself—and that part of me loves to work and make money. I had always considered working for dollars a component of my contribution to our family. I knew that I was not living a completely fulfilled life.

One day that summer after my son was born, I was talking to a real estate colleague and friend. She wanted to expand her marketing horizons, but she was so busy working **in** her business that she didn't have time to work **on** her business. She asked me what I knew about setting up a basic website. The honest answer was, "Nothing!" followed immediately by: "But I would love to figure it out for you!"

Though I didn't know it at the time, this was officially my first step toward becoming a Virtual Assistant. My friend and I agreed on a price for me to get a template website up and running for her. I did the work, sent her a bill via email, and she wrote me a check. I thought to myself: I cared for my son, worked while he slept (he was a newborn—they sleep a lot!), learned something new, and earned some decent money for my time.

Now this was something I could get used to!

I was hooked, and fortunately so was my Realtor® friend. She started having me handle more and more of the administrative aspects of her business. I was creating mailing lists, researching public records, scheduling appointments, completing paperwork, tracking closed transactions, maintaining her website, recording receipts, and more.

Along with taking on more and more responsibility for my one client, word was spreading to other Realtors® in town about the services I was offering. Other busy Realtors® started contacting me about working with them as *their* administrative assistant. I was so excited about the opportunities that I took all the work that came my way. Soon I was extremely busy—building what I would later find out was (sort of) a Virtual Assistance practice.

I say "sort of" because my business plan was seriously flawed. Actually, there was no business plan in the beginning, which was a big part of the problem. I'm not too hard on myself for not running a perfect business from the jump, though. I didn't know what I didn't know. Remember this when you start your business—do your best and always stay open to learning more and getting better at planning and running your business.

Now fast forward to 2007. I started looking toward the future of our family needs and my business. Our son was 2 and attending preschool out of the house one morning a week. The following year he would be in school 3 mornings a week and the year after he would be full time (sniffle, sniffle).

Evaluating my business, I acknowledged that I was working quite a lot and not making all that much money. Once my son was in school full time, I would need to earn a full time income. It wasn't going to happen the way I was operating my business. I'll explain "the way I was operating my business" a bit later.

I told my husband one day: I don't want to return to the traditional work force and be *that* co-worker. The co-worker that annoyed me in my younger (and dimmer) years when he/she called in sick every time his/her child was home sick, left early when his/her kid was in a school play, and took mini vacations (that they had coming) from the office all the time to keep up with snow days and summer vacation. Now that I was a parent, I knew darn well that would be me. Or worse (and this was probably my biggest fear of all), I would want the freedom over my day to still be there for my kid, and I would likely find myself **not** in a position of seniority to have that freedom. Note: yes, I **do** always want to have my cake and eat it too—and that's ok, by the way!

As a result of my fears, I made a decision that I would figure out how to strengthen my existing business. I loved being self employed, as well as the work that I was doing. It made the most sense to me to improve upon what I had already spent time and money creating. I hopped on the Internet (i.e. my second home and best friend at that time) and simply searched: "Virtual Assistance." An article from Entrepreneur magazine popped up. I skimmed the article and clicked on some of the references contained in the piece. This brought me to the website for AssistU. It was here that I learned about the definition and concept of Virtual Assistance that I'd never heard or contemplated before. I read about people that were operating **sustainable** Virtual Assistance practices. These people had fulfilled lives and were making really good livings. I learned about the Virtual

Training Program that AssistU offered and I made the decision to apply to the program.

I will never forget this part of my journey. AssistU is not an easy organization to become affiliated with. After I listened to the free information call and completed my lengthy written application, I was asked to participate in an Admissions Interview. Ok, I thought, this is good. This is where I can explain to the staff that I actually already **am** a VA, so perhaps this program isn't right for me. Huh? Why the heck was I going into this part of the process with this attitude—like I was trying to sabotage the opportunity? Because I was scared to death of my potential for greater success, of course! I was also scared to death about the cost of the tuition.

I remember coming right out of the gates in the interview explaining to the Admissions Director that a program that taught me stuff like how to use Word or

Excel was probably not something that I needed. There was a pause on the other end of the phone line and then the Admissions Director said to me very matter-of-factly: "It's assumed that you already have those skills when you join our community and go through the Virtual Training Program. What you learn in this program is, among other things, how to create and operate a sustainable business."

Uh-oh. This is exactly what I needed and wanted to move forward in my business—now what was I going to do? Remember the saying, be careful what you wish for? The next step was simple. At that moment I decided to invest in the program and more importantly myself. And boy did I ever....

By 2009, armed with a real business plan and concrete goals for myself and the business, I shifted from running a fairly successful business to operating a very a busy Virtual Assistance practice.

The difference between when I started the VA business in 2005 and when I changed the way I operated in 2009 is that my practice became **sustainable**. I was no longer was making a good living—I was making a **great** living for the hours that I was working. I started to only work with clients that I genuinely liked and was only doing work that I genuinely enjoyed. My clients worked with me on a retained, long-term basis. I knew **exactly** how much work and money I would have each month. The sky became the limit for me and my business.

Queue the next phase of the business journey.

In 2010 I noticed that more and more business owners were starting to use a marketing automation software called Infusionsoft® for their email marketing, shopping cart, and CRM (sales management). While I was learning about what this software was all about so that I could help my VA clients make informed decisions about their marketing, I fell in love with the software. I made a decision to learn everything I could about Infusionsoft®—I signed up for my own software application, attended training, and read everything I could about how and why businesses were turning to Infusionsoft for their marketing automation needs. In 2011 I made a shift to only consulting with business owners on their Infusionsoft needs. I stopped branding myself as a VA shortly after because I really do not do VA work anymore. However, I'm still very in tune with the VA industry because I help my business owner friends find good VAs to work with all the time. I also work in partnership with many VAs when I am handing off the Infusionsoft® consulting work that I have done for a business owner—VAs typically will handle the ongoing administrative support that goes with managing an Infusionsoft® application.

I've shared a large part of my journey with you in this chapter so that you can understand why I have written this book. I've spent many hours of my life feeling isolated, lost, alone, and without a professional purpose. By some stroke of luck (or whatever you want to call it) I was given an opportunity to do one small project that I barely knew how to do when I started it. Little by little I have stumbled upon good information and amazing people that have helped me build a strong business foundation.

Little. By. Little. That's why this book exists. I'm all for the philosophy that information will present itself when you are ready to receive it. However, I also know that I was looking everywhere for good, accurate, reputable information about the Virtual Assistance industry a few years ago and it was tough to find and even tougher to know what information to trust.

As Morgan Freeman said in *The Shawshank Redemption*: "Andy Dufresne, who crawled through a river of **** and came out clean on the other side."* I've written this book to save **you** some of the time and stress of swimming through the unknown. If I can make the process of learning about Virtual Assistance and starting a practice easier for even one person, I've given back to an industry that changed my life for the better in so many ways.

*http://www.imdb.com/title/tt0111161/quotes

Chapter 3
What Virtual Assistance Isn't

I often work backwards to figure things out. To figure out what I **want**, I often first figure out what I **don't want**. My husband finds it a bit annoying. However, it works like a charm, so I'll stick with the system here and recommend you give it a try as you contemplate your career plans.

First, let me tell you that if you have been wondering about what Virtual Assistance is all about, and you come away more puzzled than energized every time you try and figure it out by researching on the Internet, you're not alone. I do random Google searches pertaining to the Virtual Assistance industry every day and I know how broad the information available is.

Ah, the Internet—a Virtual Assistant's "best friend" (Don't worry all you best friends out there, your status remains safe in our lives!). In many ways, the Internet is a VA's gateway to his/her professional world. But navigating the Internet is not for the weak of heart (or lack of patience), and I believe that a person that starts their research into the Virtual Assistance industry via the Internet is bound to feel discouraged or misled, and will likely give up before they really ever get started.

In my humble opinion, the Internet is similar to the Wild West. Do you remember the Wild West in old movies and Bugs Bunny cartoons? The Wild West in those cartoons was the unknown—the land of opportunity that came loaded with headaches. It was unchartered waters where for better or worse, literally anything would go.

Combine unchartered waters with misinformation and sprinkle in a little fear; you have a colossal disaster brewing, don't you think?

The tool that gives the Virtual Assistance industry so much is also one of the biggest hurdles that Virtual Assistance encounters as a growing industry. The industry exists vastly online, and it's difficult for someone interested in learning more—whether exploring becoming a VA or exploring hiring a VA—to decipher the good, accurate information from the inaccurate. With that in mind, let me set the record straight about some common thoughts about Virtual Assistance.

Virtual Assistance isn't easy.

This may sound very obvious, but I can guarantee that a simple Internet search for "virtual assistance" will yield oodles of claims that's Virtual Assistance—and any job working from home for that matter—is easy peasy. In a nutshell: no way.

Running a Virtual Assistance practice, like running **any** business, takes a lot of work. Not in a bad way. At a minimum, building a sustainable Virtual Assistance practice will require **writing and following a business plan, marketing**, and **networking**. Then, when you are done doing these things on a regular basis (hint: marketing and networking has become very important if you want to build a full practice), you will have client work to manage. If you plan, market, and network effectively, you will have **a lot** of client work if you want it. Operating a Virtual Assistance practice takes time, talent, and dedication to your plan. Like everything else in life, nothing worth anything starts out easy, and running a business is no exception.

Virtual Assistance isn't a hobby.

Since I have so much flexibility in my schedule and I very often have a big smile on my face and in my voice (a dear friend of mine often lovingly refers to me as a "Pollyanna" on Facebook), people often assume that I merely dabble in work. I don't just think this; I **know** that many people don't think I work very much. Perhaps I should be offended one of these days, but really I'm not. Instead, I'm thrilled. It reinforces what I know about building and running a business that you love: you can joyfully make a very good living while everyone you know thinks you have nothing but free time. What a win-win! When you are making a living and no one even knows it you really must have your business down pat!

The reality is that my flex schedule and happy disposition is because I **LOVE** what I do. You will never love your Virtual Assistance if you dabble. You won't ever love (or be good at) anything if you only dabble. There is no money in dabbling!

Virtual Assistance isn't the right or best career choice for everyone.

On the one hand, you could feasibly open up a VA practice tomorrow. You don't need a license, permit, or permission from anyone to do so. On the other hand, you can **never** operate a VA practice if you are not qualified to do so. You need a high level of administrative skills, passion for your work, and a strong desire to own your own business.

When you see ads and articles online that generally state that "you" can be a Virtual Assistant and start making lots and lots of money "today" consider this: if it were that simple, wouldn't **everyone** be a VA?

Virtual Assistance isn't a get rich quick scheme.

I have a Yahoo email account that I use as a non-professional option, and it never fails that every day I receive "emails" (it's email but really it's spam) letting me know 1. I have a free computer waiting for me somewhere, and 2. There is a work from home opportunity awaiting me that pays thousands upon thousands of dollars per week. I don't open either of these emails, and these two examples are examples of get rich quick schemes, of which Virtual Assistance is not.

You can make a very good living as a VA, but you **work** for every dime you bill to a client. You use your own office equipment, you pay your own taxes, you pay for your own marketing and advertising, and you depend on **you** to network with prospective clients. There is no magic pill to put together a thriving VA practice, and really, why should there be? All reputable businesses take hard work and planning, and Virtual Assistance is no exception.

Virtual Assistance isn't a cheap alternative to an employee.

Wouldn't that be nice! I love a bargain as much as anyone else, but growing a business is far too serious an endeavor to misunderstand this area of the Virtual Assistance business model.

Virtual Assistants are not a bargain administrative assistant option. A business owner that really needs the presence and time commitment of an in house employee to meet the needs of his/her business should never consider a VA as their core source for administrative assistance. They should instead hire an employee and pay them a salary, provide an office, equipment, and benefits.

If a business owner interviews you because he/she is trying to **hire** a VA solely to save money (i.e. not pay taxes, health insurance, overtime, overhead...), run the other direction because the partnership will not last long—if it ever comes together at all.

On the other hand, a business owner that wants to *partner* with an administrative professional that will step in and be of equal importance in determining the business's onward and upward success, they are quite possibly the ideal client for a VA.

A VA is not "cheap" (I discuss fees in another chapter), but the VA business model is the most efficient option a small business owner can consider. When working with a Virtual Assistant a business owner does need to budget for things such as additional office space, taxes, benefits, and down time. A VA also "shows up" (virtually speaking) with the knowledge and experience needed to get right to work. Efficiency and value far outweigh a Virtual Assistant's fee.

A Virtual Assistant isn't always the right choice for a business owner.

There are plenty of situations that warrant the need for an in-house, full time administrative **employee**. If you are a highly skilled administrative professional and you finish this book and decide that operating your own Virtual Assistance practice isn't for you, no worries as there will always be a need for your valued (and invaluable) skills in the traditional work place. As a matter of fact, while researching for an article that I was writing, I found this statistic: "Secretaries and administrative assistants held more than 4.2 million jobs in 2006, ranking it among the largest occupations in the US economy…Employment of secretaries and administrative assistants is expected to increase about 9% between 2006 and 2016...."*

The above information was gathered prior to the economic decline that we faced beginning in 2008, but it's safe to assume there is still a tremendous need for administrative professionals in the traditional work place.

*http://www.bls.gov/oco/ocos151.htm

A Virtual Assistant isn't all knowing.

A qualified and quality (these are two separate traits, by the way) Virtual Assistant possesses a massive amount of administrative knowledge. However, no human ever knows everything—and that includes Virtual Assistants. A good VA knows where to find the people or the information that can fill the knowledge gaps when they appear.

Additionally, a good VA only does work that he/she enjoys doing. That will undoubtedly mean that there will be things the client needs done that the VA doesn't do (I didn't do extensive phone work when I was running my VA business, for example). This is another example of when a VA uses their knowledge and networking to suggest alternative professionals to handle the needs that the VA can't, or doesn't wish to, handle.

A Virtual Assistant isn't ever on standby.

This was how I operated my VA practice when I started out and it was a big reason why I wasn't making any money.

If a client pops in and out of your life once or twice or three times a year, you will never, ever be able to plan a stable schedule of time or money for yourself and your business.

Working this way also never lets a VA really get to know a client. You never really get a glimpse at what your client's business needs are because you have no idea what they are doing or how they are doing it. There is no thrill to swooping in and doing 2 hours of work per year for a client; and you will work yourself into a frenzy peppered with disappointment and exhaustion if you try to operate a business (any business) this way.

I hope you are not discouraged because I just told you about a whole bunch about what a Virtual Assistant **is not**. Instead, you should be more excited than ever. I have pointed out all of the annoying things that VA business owners sometimes find themselves encountering as they are trying to start and grow a business and I have already prepared you to plan to set standards and boundaries for your business around these things. It's like reading the last page of a book before you have read it—consider my experiences stumbling over and through ALL of the things mentioned in this chapter as a time saver! Onward!

Chapter 4
What Virtual Assistance Is

Ok, now that we got **that** out of the way, let's talk about what this fabulous industry is **really** all about!

I once had the privilege of interviewing Stacy Brice, Founder and Chief Visionary Officer at AssistU for a newsletter article that I was writing. Stacy, in my opinion and the opinion of many others, created the Virtual Assistance business model in the 1980's. She went on to start a program called the Virtual Training Program in the 1990's that I will discuss in another chapter.

This was the definition of Virtual Assistance that Stacy shared with me during our interview:

"I define Virtual Assistance as providing administrative and personal support in long term collaborative relationships without being in the same location as the client."

Stacy Brice
President, Chief Visionary Officer
AssistU
www.assistu.com

Here are some additional thoughts about what Virtual Assistance **is**:

A Virtual Assistant is a small business owner.

In a nutshell, this means that you are self-employed when you are a Virtual Assistant. This could mean different things to different people (depending on many factors such as what state you live in). For me, it meant that I didn't receive a W2 from any of my clients. In turn I was solely responsible for paying my taxes. I still am, by the way, I just have my company structured a little bit differently now than I did when I was first starting out with a Virtual Assistance business.

The best advice I can give in this area is to **consult with your Accountant** (and if you don't have one, it's time to get one) before you take on your first client so that when you get paid, you're handling everything correctly. Issues as simple as "do I have to set up a separate bank account for my VA practice?" are things that you need to iron out with your tax professional.

A Virtual Assistant is a highly skilled administrative professional with a broad skill set.

- ✓ PDF conversion? Check.

- ✓ Editing & Proofreading? Check.

- ✓ Schedule management? Check.

- ✓ Email management? Check.

- ✓ Processing payments? Check.

- ✓ Internet research? Check.

- ✓ Travel arrangements? Check.

- ✓ Expense reports? Check.

- ✓ Invoicing? Check.

- ✓ Setting appointments? Check.

- ✓ Obtaining customer feedback? Check.

- ✓ Processing orders and requests? Check.

- ✓ Setting up a Facebook Page? Check?

- ✓ Setting up a Twitter Page? Check.

- ✓ Setting up a LinkedIn page? Check.

- ✓ Managing Social Media using a tool like Hootsuite? Check.

- ✓ Blog updates? Check.

✓ Microsoft Word, Excel, PowerPoint and beyond? Check…

✓ Insert **your** favorite work here!

Really, there is no test to determine whether a person is qualified and ready to be a successful Virtual Assistant. But it's safe to say that if **none** of the information in the list above rings a bell or resonates with you, you aren't ready to take on clients.

A Virtual Assistant works **with** clients.

Generally speaking, we (as a society, and particularly in the United States) are used to the traditional employer/employee or boss/worker relationship. This is how business typically operates in the traditional workplace: someone works **for** someone else.

This is not the case in the land of Virtual Assistance. A VA and his/her client are **equals** in the working relationship. Neither person works **for** the other person. On a basic level, a self-employed person can't engage in an employer/employee relationship (if they want to remain self employed in the government's eyes).

Instead we often refer to our working relationship as a partnership. When you think of yourself as a partner in an endeavor, you naturally become more interested in seeing a successful outcome.

A Virtual Assistant sets his/her own hours, fees, and operating standards.

This is your business and you're the boss of you. You determine everything that happens in your business. Hours, fees, and standards vary throughout the industry based on the individual needs and goals of the VA.

Let's start with hours. If you work best in the morning, have morning business hours. If you want to structure your day to parallel most of your client's office hours, go for it. If you prefer an opposite schedule to your clients—and that arrangement is ok with you and your clients—then consider clients in other time zones. If you live in the Central Time Zone and you have a client in, say, England, there is a 7 hour time difference making this type of set up possible. Even the difference between a Virtual Assistant in California and a client in New York is vast enough to make opposite schedules work.

Some clients LOVE the idea of their VA working when they are done for the day.

In theory, this set-up allows their businesses to "run" many more hours each day than if there was just one person handling everything.

Tip: Time zones can be tricky (especially when you have multiple clients in multiple time zones!) so consider a conversion table to ensure everyone is on the same "page." I actually have 4 clocks on a wall in my office. Each one is set to a different time zone. The mass ticking took some getting used to, but I have not mixed up a time zone since.

Fees are always a "hot" topic. The short answer is, your fees will depend upon many factors, and I'll touch a little more on fees in a later chapter.

Operating standards are again determined by each VA and vary greatly. Standards include determining your billing procedure, determining how you stay in touch with clients each week, expectations of clients, and what clients may expect from you. This is all information you can, and should, put in your business plan.

A Virtual Assistant is able to work with several different clients at a time.

A VA can work with as many small business owners as they like and their work load will allow. Some VAs fill their practice with one client and others may work with upwards of 10 clients—all of whom need just a few hours per month (5-10 hours / month, for example). How a VA decides to structure his/her practice is totally the VA's call—the beauty of running your own business!

A Virtual Assistant is mobile.

You can work pretty much anywhere you can get a **secure** Internet connection when you are a Virtual Assistant. I have an office in my home, I have an office at my second home, and I have a laptop computer that allows me to take my business anywhere, anytime.

Tip: If you plan to have a mobile lifestyle, seriously consider getting an Aircard of Mifi connection as an Internet connection option to use when you are working outside of your office. An Aircard or a Mifi is a piece of equipment (and an additional service) that you obtain through a cell phone company that provides Internet service.

To clarify "an additional service," I pay for my cell phone plan AND my Mifi plan on my cell phone bill each month.
Typically, you will follow the same procedure to obtain an Aircard or a Mifi

as you do when getting a cell phone: purchase the equipment, commit to a contract, and pay monthly for service.

I emphasized **secure** earlier in this section because when you are working on client work, you don't want to ever do so via an unsecured Internet connection. Public places that offer "Free Wifi" are often an unsecured Internet connection, for example. You will never want to risk your client's work being seen by the wrong eyes or fall into the wrong hands.

Another way to look at the mobility that Virtual Assistance offers is to "take your show on the road," so to speak, and bring yourself and your services to local clients. If you are drawn to the idea of local clients and working outside of your home office and often face-to-face with your clients, this is a business model to consider. The Virtual Assistant that I consider the industry leader when it comes to this business model is Angela

Mattson of Define Your Day. Visit her website (click on the hyperlink in the previous sentence) to learn more about operating as a mobile VA!

A Virtual Assistant is considered "full time" if operating their VA practice is their only job.

In the traditional workplace, someone is considered "full time" if they work (typically) 40 hours per week. It's not the same with operating a Virtual Assistance practice. For marketing purposes, a VA is "full time" as long as their practice is their only work—whether it's 10 hours per month or 100. Conversely, a VA's practice is considered part time when the VA has another job in addition to operating the VA practice.

A Virtual Assistant controls his/her own destiny.

When I said earlier in this book that the sky is the limit for my business, I meant that for **everyone** that operates a Virtual Assistance practice. When you operate a VA practice you can work with as many clients as you want. You can work with whomever you want. You can work any hours you want. You can work any days that you want. You can market yourself as a generalist or you can focus on one profession as your potential clients (Authors, Coaches, Realtors, etc.).

As you and your VA practice grow, you may find you have interests in addition to working with clients. As an example, I love to work with clients, and I also love to write, speak, teach and mentor. Since I'm my own boss, I structure my time and my businesses to allow me the opportunity to do all (and only) the things I want to do—isn't life grand?!

Chapter 5
Starting A VA Practice

As I said previously, you can technically launch a Virtual Assistance practice tomorrow. Actually, you can put this book down (though I hope you finish it first), head over to your computer, hop online and announce to the world that you are a Virtual Assistant. You don't need a "VA license" (though you may need a license to operate a small business in your community, so be sure to do your homework) or a degree or certification to open your virtual doors. You need your skills and abilities—as an administrative professional, business person, and marketer to get started. In a way, I sort of did that. And as I shared, that approach didn't get me very far, financially.

Business training is optional but **highly** recommended. There are many Virtual Assistance training options available online (do an Internet search for "virtual assistance training" to see what I mean). As I said before, the Internet is a very broad place, and not all options are as reputable as others. I will list a handful of options that I know are reputable and whose products are worthy of your time to research further.

Please note: If a training option that currently exists is NOT included in this book it does not necessarily mean that the option isn't reputable or worth your time and resources. I have included options that I can vouch for based on my personal experience. **The bottom line: always do your homework before investing in anything.** Consider this a good jumping off point for that research.

Launch Your Virtual Assistance Business in 30 Day (OR LESS!)

This is a home study program that I created that, unlike this book, will take you through the practical steps of planning launching a Virtual Assistance business. I used to teach this class live (online) and now offer all of the great information in a home study program. Visit jessicamaes.com/30-day-va-home-study-course/ for more details.

The Virtual Basics Program from AssistU

You will recall I described a live, 20 week program that I participated in at AssistU in 2008. That program is no longer available and this home study option is available in its place. Learn all about the program by visiting http://www.assistu.com/va/training/.

The Virtual Assistance Chamber of Commerce (VACOC) has many useful forms available for purchase that will help you plan and operate a successful VA practice.

The organization called VA Networking (VAnetworking.com) also offers a self-study option.

One thing that all of the above options will do for you: they all will give you step-by-step direction to start and operate a sustainable VA practice.

Chapter 6
Finding Clients

I remember a time when I had a fear of not finding clients. As Oprah says, "When you know better you do better"—isn't that the truth? Now I know better. When I say that clients are everywhere, I'm not kidding. I know it sounds like I'm oversimplifying things, but I give this simple answer every time I'm asked because it's the truth!

I shared with you in an earlier chapter how I connected with my first client—a friend that I had worked with 3 years prior. I have found many of my other clients through word of mouth—good news travels fast! I have worked with business owners that I know from my neighborhood. I have connected with potential clients on Internet social networking sites like Facebook, Twitter and LinkedIn. People have found me via my website. When I was still operating a Virtual Assistance practice, I was considered an AssistU graduate in good standing so I was able to subscribe to the AssistU Registry which provides many pre-qualified leads (i.e. requests from small business owners looking for a VA) per month.

The other way to find clients that we often never think of because we are building an online company: traditional networking. There was a time when I feared networking—getting out from behind my computer and coming outside, in my car, over to an event and actually talking to people. But let me tell you this: the Virtual Assistants that do this are swimming in clients. Granted, you can't just show up, business card in hand, and expect to fill your practice in one swoop. It's really all about building relationships and that takes time, effort, commitment, follow up, and discipline.

But the takeaway is this: networking with business owners in your community can work when you are building a Virtual Assistance business.

If you asked other VAs they would probably give the same answers and offer a few other creative examples. As a matter of fact, I went ahead and did just that. Here is what some of my VA colleagues had to share when I asked them how where they have found clients:

"I was in a local master mind group with some other small business owners in my community. I started chatting with a fellow member and we learned that I could do a lot to help her with the administrative side of her business. We also learned that we liked each other a lot, so it helped us make the decision to work together."

Gretchen Christy
GC Virtual Support
www.gcvirtualsupport.com

"Four of my clients are people that I already knew before they became clients. That in itself is good news for aspiring VAs. I have also interviewed three different potential clients as a result of networking on Twitter. Bottom line: it's impossible to know who needs your services and who doesn't – talk to everyone about your business!"

Amy Kinnaird
ArK Virtual
www.arkvirtual.com

"I was blessed to get another client via "volunteering". Not just for anything, but for a "stretch" assignment. It was partnering with someone more experienced than I was and while I lent my expertise, I learned a great deal

along the way. As time went by, I was seen as a leader and coach and was asked to be the facilitator for their Board of Directors. They have hired me and retained me as a Board Liaison (one of my signature Virtual Partner programs). My hours volunteering definitely paid off!"

Tiffany Odutoye
Virtual Partner, LLC
www.virtualpartner.biz

The common theme here is that potential clients are everywhere, and once you are set up and confident about your Virtual Assistance practice, you simply need to start talking (a lot) about your business—it's amazing what happens!

Chapter 7
Technology & Virtual Assistance

Technology is a Virtual Assistant's best friend. VAs work remotely, so most client work needs to be done via phone, fax, snail mail, email, and via the Internet—with a major emphasis on "email and via the Internet"!

So much of the technology that small business owners use is web based. The software lives on the Internet and users log in to access the information. This means the information can be accessed via the client's office, the VA's office, as well as all or none of the above. The log-in and password information is what keeps the information safe and secure on the Internet (along with various

Internet security measures that companies with web based software provide to users).

Another technology concept that many VAs and their clients employ is shared workspaces. Shared workspaces are often web based, and sometimes free, software that more than one person can access and share information on. A VA can upload a document from his/her office to the workspace; the client can access the file in the workspace, edit and save back to the workspace for the VA to access further.

Remote access is another concept that VAs and clients often use to work together. With remote desktop access, one computer (usually the client's) has software loaded on to it and then another user on another computer (usually the VA) can log in to the computer with the remote desktop software on it. It's a nifty way for a VA to remotely be present in his/her client's office.

There are far too many technology options available to Virtual Assistants to list in this chapter. The important thing to do when you become a VA is to keep your eyes and ears open and learn as much as you can online. Clients rely on their VA for guidance and suggestions on best practices for their partnership. The more you know, or are willing to learn, the better off you and your clients will be.

In no particular order, here are some examples of technology that VAs use frequently, many **every day**:

✓ Outlook and Gmail

✓ Microsoft Word and Excel, and PowerPoint

✓ MyHours – www.myhours.com

- ✓ LogMeIn – www.logmein.com

- ✓ QuickBooks – www.quickbooks.com

- ✓ DropBox – www.dropbox.com

- ✓ Wordpress – www.wordpress.com and www.wordpress.org

- ✓ Facebook – www.facebook.com

- ✓ Twitter – www.twitter.com

- ✓ LinkedIn – www.linkedin.com

- ✓ Hootsutie – www.hootsuite.com

- ✓ iContact - www.iContact.com

- ✓ Constant Contact – www.constantcontact.com

- ✓ Paypal – www.paypal.com

- ✓ FreeConferencePro –
  www.freeconferencepro.com

- ✓ Basecamp –
  www.basecamphq.com

- ✓ GotToMeeting and GoToWebinar
  – www.gotomeeting.com

- ✓ Infusionsoft –
  www.infusionsoft.com

- ✓ 1ShoppingCart – www.1sc.com

- ✓ GoDaddy – www.godaddy.com

- ✓ 1and1 – www.1and1.com

And many, many, many more!

Chapter 8
Frequently Asked Questions

Here are many Frequently Asked Questions about the Virtual Assistance industry that have not been addressed at any length in previous chapters.

How many hours does a VA work?

You determine how many hours you work, but generally a full time VA with a full practice will work upwards of 100 hours per month.

I know that's *only* 25 hours per week. You might have thought that "full time" was 40 hours per week. In the corporate world, full time often *is* upwards of 40 hours per week (which often turns into 50-60 hours per week when you add in work load and commute, right?). The 25 hours per week I mention here are **billable hours**. This is the **actual time** spent working on a client's business. This does not include, for example, bathroom breaks, lunch hour, non-business related phone calls or non-business time on the Internet. You will work upwards of 40 hours per week in this scenario, but the additional hours will be time spent working **on** your business rather than **in** your business.

As an aside, 100 hours per month is **a lot**. Some of the most successful VAs that I know choose to bill about 80 hours per month.

How many clients does a VA work with at a time?

I find the answer to this question is more a matter of hours than clients. Typically a VA determines how many hours they wish to work in the practice per month, and then fills the practice with clients that have live needs, hours-wise.

Example: if a VA decides he/she will consider their practice full at 80 hours per month, they may work with 4 clients at 20 hours per month each, or 3 clients at 20 hours per month each and 2 clients at 10 hours per month each, or…you get the idea.

Can I operate a VA practice part time and have a full time "day job"?

Absolutely! The Virtual Assistance business model is very flexible, and really whatever works for you and your clients is what matters.

Generally speaking, the industry defines a full time VA as a Virtual Assistant who only operates a VA practice as their career. A part time VA works another job in addition to operating a VA practice. This is different from the traditional definitions of full and part time.

How much do VAs charge?

In my experience, this is by far the most popular question asked by aspiring VAs as well as business owners who are considering partnering with a VA.

There is no one answer to this question. Every VA sets his/her own fees, and fees are generally based on the VA's experience and the costs they incur (i.e. overhead) to run their business. You really have to create a budget for your business to have an understanding of how much you need to charge to make your business sustainable. You usually create a budget when you write your business plan.

Generally speaking, a VA typically charges somewhere between $35-$90+/hour for their services.

I'm a great administrative assistant, but I'm shy. Do I have to go to "networking" events to find clients?

Whether you're shy or you simply don't enjoy traditional networking events (such as a Chamber of Commerce meeting), know that you don't have to market at traditional networking events if you don't feel comfortable doing so.

However, I have found that this is a skill—getting over the shyness and attending live networking events—worth mastering. Truth be told, I'm not comfortable at events like that, and I didn't attend live networking events very much in the early years of my business. It all worked out ok for me, but I now know that I could have grown my business faster if I would have faced this fear of shyness (and rejection!) and participated in live networking events.

Whatever you decide to do about networking, know this: as a business owner, you must market yourself and your business and you must network. You can determine how you plan to do these things when you craft your business plan.

Do Virtual Assistants carry insurance?

You would need to consult with a business insurance agent to determine what type of insurance you need to carry to operate a VA practice from your home office. Rules vary depending on what State you live in and what insurance company you insure with.

Do Virtual Assistants operate as sole proprietors, or something else?

This is a question for your Accountant. Some Virtual Assistants operate as a sole proprietor, some as an LLC, and some as a Corporation. Like insurance, this is a question best left to the respective professionals.

Does a VA get W2s from each client at the end of the year?

W2s are issued by employers, and VA clients **are not** employers. When you meet with your Accountant to discuss your business, be sure to discuss W2s,

1099s, and any other year end forms that your clients may ask you about.

Do you need a separate/special bank account to run your VA practice?

The answer to this may vary depending on the state you live in, and it may also depend on what business status you choose for your business (see previous question). I personally have business bank accounts, and would have it no other way. I always assumed that business bank accounts were fancy and expensive, but I found great, affordable products at my local credit union. I have had clients tell me that they have found similar products at their respective banks. The key is to check around (no pun intended).

Do Virtual Assistants ever take a vacation?

Of course! You can block out as much "out of the office" time as you wish—it's **your** business! Be sure to work out whatever you plan to do with your clients as far in advance as you can as a matter of courtesy and professionalism. Some Virtual Assistants have a colleague handle things for them while they are gone. Others simply put their involvement in their client's businesses on hold until they return to the office.

Can you operate a Virtual Assistance practice with kids in the house?

Again, it's your business and you can operate however you wish. When my son was a baby I was able to work around his schedule (when he was sleeping). As he got more active I hired a babysitter to come to the house to care for him while I worked in my home office. Now I work when he is in school.

If you do plan to have active kids in your charge while you work, I feel it's best to let your clients know this as a courtesy. If you plan to do work that involves being on the phone, it may be very difficult/possibly unprofessional to work with kids in your charge.

Does a VA ever turn away business?

A successful VA will eventually have to say "no thank you" to a prospective client. Not every prospective client will be the right "fit" for your practice. You may not be wild about the prospective client and/or the work that they would like a VA to handle for them. In my experience, when faced with a less than ideal opportunity, it's best in the long run to politely decline.

A VA will also eventually have a full practice by virtue of there not being any more hours in the work day. When your practice is full, you will likely have to decline opportunities or at least start a waiting list for future openings.

Overall: Let's face it, calling your own shots and having a full practice are very exciting "problems" to have!

Do I need a certification to be a VA?

No, you don't. However, home study programs to help you take the next step and start planning a Virtual Assistance business are very helpful and worth your consideration. I listed a few options for this in Chapter 5.

Do VAs ever have VAs as clients?

Yes! **All** small business owners potentially need a VA, and Virtual Assistants are no exception. I speak from experience because I have a VA that works with me to grow the teaching, speaking, and writing part of my business. As a matter of fact, if not for my VA, this book wouldn't be in front of you right now—she gets things done that I'd still be working on 6 months from now!

Some VAs also partner with a VA to operate their VA practice. This could mean working on the VA's client's work, and it could also mean working on the business side of the VA's business (i.e. billing, marketing, etc.).

Who needs a VA?

Overall, the thing to remember is that as a Virtual Assistant you can potentially work with *any* small business owner whose work resonates with you—the options are limitless!

Here are examples (it's a teeny tiny list, but a good start) of small business owners that partner with Virtual

Assistants for their administrative business needs:

- Realtors®
- Attorneys
- Virtual Assistants
- Business Coaches
- Life Coaches
- Authors
- Intuitives
- Speakers
- Financial Planners
- Inventors
- Accountants
- Appraisers
- Marketing Experts
- **Any** small business owner that needs assistance in order to spend their entire day doing **only** the work that they love and that makes them money.

Are you hiring?

This is another common question that a VA receives. As you know by this point in the book, VAs typically do not hire employees—we are solopreneurs and we tend to work with other solopreneurs.

Chapter 9
Where To Find More Information

You have come a long way in this book and have hopefully learned a lot about what this industry is all about. If you remain intrigued or better yet, interested at this point, it's time to head to the Internet and do some more research. Here is a list of web sites I suggest you review to learn more about the Virtual Assistance industry:

www.assistu.com

www.virtualassistantnetworking.com

www.VAnetworking.com

www.wisconsinvanetwork.com

www.facebook.com - There are tons of VAs on Facebook. Find them, add them to your friends, and network with them to learn more. While you are there, reconnect with old friends – it's lots of fun!

www.twitter.com - There are tons of VAs on Twitter, too. Find them, follow them, and network to learn more.

www.linkedin.com - There are many VAs on LinkedIn, and there are also many work-from-home and VA specific groups that you can join and learn more.

This list will give you a good, solid start. By searching each site you will find other sites and people to research. Find out all you can—it's all part of smart, responsible business planning!

Chapter 10
Closing – What's Next?

The next step is up to **you**....

If you are jumping up and down with excitement over what you have learned in this book about Virtual Assistance, then the industry most definitely has resonated with you and you should seriously consider taking steps toward writing a solid business plan.

If you've realized this isn't really something you are all that interested in now that you've learned more, consider giving this book to a friend to read. Very often people say something isn't for them, but that their sister (or friend, mother, brother, cousin, neighbor...) would be a perfect VA. Whether this information resonates with you or not, it's good, useful information all the same and should be shared.

Virtual Assistance is still a young industry, and it needs as much solid support as it can get to help the industry grow bigger and stronger. One way or another, **you** can be instrumental in that growth!

Thank you for taking the time to learn more about an industry that's near and dear to me. If you have further questions, never hesitate to reach out to me via email: jessica@jessicamaes.com.

DISCLAIMER:
The views and opinions expressed in this ebook are based on the author's personal experiences, but cannot be relied on to produce any specific results. The success of any business venture, including that of a virtual assistant, depends on many factors including the diligence and hard work of the owner. There are no representations or warranties, either expressed or implied, concerning the outcome of following any of the steps.

About The Author

Jessica Maes launched Maes Consulting in 2005 as a Virtual Assistance business that provided general administrative support to small business owners. Identifying a need in the marketplace for focused marketing strategy and support, Jessica Maes shifted the company's focus to providing Infusionsoft strategy and support to businesses worldwide.

Committed to providing the best Infusionsoft consulting to the marketplace, Jessica earned the Infusionsoft Certified Consultant designation in 2011. The ICC designation is an intense week of instruction at the Infusionsoft Headquarters and includes a rigorous exam.

After earning her Bachelor's degree in English in 3½ years from the University of Wisconsin–Parkside, Jessica worked in several industries including real estate, insurance, retail, and banking.

Jessica is committed to education which is why she has created learning and mentoring programs for aspiring Virtual Assistants and administrative professionals who wish to provide Infusionsoft support to business owners. Jessica is a co-founder of the Wisconsin VA Network, author of *Exploring A Career As A Virtual Assistant* and co-author of a book about Infusionsoft software best practices that will be available in 2012.

Jessica lives in Madison, Wisconsin, where she cheers on the Packers and Badgers with her husband and son. She also enjoys knitting, hiking, and traveling.

Special Thanks

Kevin and Henry – You guys are why I get out of bed in the morning.

Anna Trull – My first VA client and my dear friend.

Stacy Brice – Thank you for AssistU—I t changed my life.

Gretchen Christy – Colleague & friend.

Rachel Rasmussen & Melodee Patterson—Fellow co-founders of the Wisconsin Virtual Assistant Network.

Mary Jean Ruhnke – For giving my live VA class a shot.

Amy Kinnaird – My first VA and now my favorite social media evangelist and accountability partner.

Kris Cunningham – 1st Edition editor extraordinaire.

Meghan Engsberg Cunningham – 2nd Edition editor extraordinaire.

Made in the USA
Monee, IL
13 December 2024

73554278R00056